MOVING AS TWO

A GUIDE FOR BALLROOM DANCERS
LOOKING FOR BALANCE, POWER, FREEDOM
AND HARMONY IN PARTNERSHIP

BY SUSANNA HARDT

Moving as Two: A Guide For Ballroom Dancers looking
for balance, power, freedom, and harmony in partnership

Photo by Drew Altizer
Photo of Susanna Hardt and Todd Marsden

Printed in the United States of America
ISBN 9780615659893

ACKNOWLEDGMENTS

I am indebted to my copy editor and mother, Lois Hardt, whose time and careful attention made this book much clearer and cleaner than it would have been. Thank you to my husband and dance partner Todd Marsden for his many insightful edits. Thanks to my journalist editor and sister Dr. Heidi Hardt as well as to fellow competitors Heather Brockett and Sunny Williams for their helpful feed-back. I am greatly appreciative of my ballroom teachers, ballroom champions Tomas Atkocevicius and Aira Bubnelyte, for their tireless patience and creativity in describing abstract concepts and for passing down the wisdom of their great ballroom teachers, Richard Gleave, Ann Gleave, Janet Gleave, Michael and Vicki Barr, and John Wood. Thank you also to the dance professionals who encouraged me in the early stages to write this book, Andrea Nelson Novak cofounder of Bay West Ballroom and Diane Jarmolow, founder of the Ballroom Dance Teachers College. Thank you also for the support of my first ballroom dance teachers, Tom and Eileen Fitzpatrick who gave me confidence and taught me to "stand up tall". I am very thankful for my writing group led by Leslie Keenan for their support, feedback, and encouragement. This book would not have been completed without them. Finally, thanks to this book, that persistently insisted, against all internal resistences, that it be written.

CONTENTS

*

NOTE TO THE READER:

This book is to help you. It is to make things simpler - in dance and in your life.

In ballroom dancing, sometimes it seems there are so many things to remember, so many instructions to follow, so many possible mistakes, so many complications. Here is a basic little framework that you can pour in all the little things you learn.

This is it. Because there are some simple truths in dance and if you know them and just keep coming back to them, you are all set.

This is also a book on mindfulness, about paying attention, because ballroom is a path to mindfulness, as is paying attention a way to improve your ballroom.

It is a book about developing successful and satisfying partnerships, about avoiding unnecessary distractions, and about noticing and using the power that is in you and your body. It is a reminder to stay on the right and most efficient path towards improving yourself and your quality of movement.

The following are your dance instructions. Treat them with care, protect them, clean them, dust them off. Make them true to you. But most of all see and experience each very clearly. It is the bringing these elements together in your body that will bring you balance, freedom, and harmony in partnership.

INTRODUCTION

This book can be used in different ways by different audiences. The beginning dancer can use the principals in this book in conjunction with classes and lessons as a kind of basic grammar of how movement works in partnership. The exercises at the end of the chapter will be helpful in developing a bodily understanding of each of these elements. For the more advanced dancer, this book is a way both to assemble what you may already know in a useful package of reminders and to offer some specific suggestions for training that can smooth out your path of development in partnership.

In traditional ballroom dance literature, often partners are referred to as "man" and "lady." As more and more same-sex partners are dancing ballroom, in some literature partners are referred to as "leader" and "follower." The essential principals of movement in partnership are the same for both partners in a couple regardless of gender or role. I mean each of the elements of this book to apply to you, so please replace the genders as you see fit.

There are many essential details of ballroom dancing that are outside the scope of this book, but have been well described in writings by others. A recommended reading list at the end of the book includes titles of books which discuss important subjects such as usage of feet, degrees of turn, rise and fall, body position, specific dance figures, and choreography.

I wanted a simple book that would remind us of the most basic principals of movement in partnership, that we can come back to again and again until gradually these principals are taken on as habits for our body, and our movement in relationships gets easier. I hope that it will be helpful to you and your dancing.

PART ONE

PREPARATION:

GET INTO YOUR BODY &

CONCENTRATE YOUR MIND

It is important to recognize that the state of your mind and body coming into practice is almost as important to the development of your dancing as the dancing itself. With that said, I'd like to take a moment to discuss preparation.

It seems perhaps a bit obvious to say that you need to be in your body when you are trying to develop as a dancer, but our modern lives are an increasingly out-of-body string of experiences, in which our mind drags our body along for the ride from one thing to the next thing to Get Things Done! We are rarely aware of our bodies, and, when we are, the awareness is minimal, just enough to tell them to do something they usually do not want to do, or when something hurts. We rarely listen just to hear what they have to say. We love to dance, because bodies naturally love to dance. But, competition ballroom dancing, or Dancesport, is something more; it involves wanting to develop and refine our movement so that we become more efficient as movers and so that we can do and express what we really want to express to our audiences. As such, it involves giving up some bad habits and thus that we are aware that we have bad habits to begin with. This is a challenging enterprise and if we are to undertake it, it is best to develop a quality relationship with our body, so that it is more likely to accommodate the things we would like to do with it.

Before we begin there is something we must understand, namely that we are not our body or, rather, what we assume our body will do on any particular day is not in fact what it will do on any particular day. Each day it may feel a bit different. It may be capable of doing different things. Sometimes it feels sore and achy and like it cannot do much of anything, and then once we warm up a little, it does great things. Other days it feels great and immediately does everything we ask of it. We must check in and find out how it is doing today at this moment.

Also it is helpful as you train to notice where your body may have weaknesses, so that you can give your body in advance whatever particular supplemental exercises or warm-ups it may need to stay strong and flexible.

We are biological creatures and we must nurture our

bodies and train them as such. It is helpful to think of your body as a horse in training. Your body will need patience, guidance, and persistence. So it is you and your body/horse that will go into practice together. Knowing this will help immensely with your expectations of how you will progress.

Breathe

The first step to engaging our connection with our own bodies is to find a quiet space to sit or stand where you won't be disturbed and to take a few moments to feel your breath. Breathe deeply and consciously. Then take a moment to listen to what your body is telling you. Is it sore, tight, tired? What shape is it taking right now? Move your body around a little and feel what else it may have to say. By taking a moment to listen to our bodies, it is easier for parts of our body to coordinate with each other, and, as a result, for us to move in the way we want to move. Also, once we have brought our awareness into our own body, it is much easier to be aware of things outside of ourselves, such as the music, our partner, and the space of the ballroom. If you find difficulty sensing what your body feels, see the body scan exercise in the Sample Practice chapter at the end of the book to help yourself listen a bit more deeply.

Once you can hear what your body has to say, then you can begin to request things for it to do. And when you have requested it to do something, you will need to listen and see if it is doing what you have asked of it.

Concentrating mind

Your mind in ballroom dancing should work like your breath. You are constantly breathing in, taking in information from your body, your partner, your surroundings, and then breathing out, directing your body to do something, actively producing something on the dance floor. So, both sides of your mind need to be constantly engaged, the one side that you tend to use to listen and notice things and the side that tends to direct or instruct your body to do things. It is up to you to keep an even back and forth so that you are almost doing both simultaneously.

The process of tuning into your body and hearing what your body has to say has the automatic advantage of concentrating your mind, which, like your body, does not always do what you would like it to do. When you arrive to practice, your mind is often still elsewhere and takes a bit of time to focus on the task at hand. It often is caught in thoughts or emotions from the day. Getting into your body calms the mind and reminds it what its task is to do at this moment.

There has been much written on mindfulness and the advantages of being truly present in each moment. Suffice it to say that the more you are able to be present during your practice, the more you will reap the rewards.

Try:

See how much of your body you can feel at this moment and see how much you can be inside of it. Check in briefly before practice. Is there anything your body wants to say to you? What is contracted, stretched, tight, open? Where is your sense of balance? Do you feel heavy, light? Move around to the music. Can you sense where you are in space?

PART TWO

YOU AS AN INDIVIDUAL: BALANCED, POWERFUL, AND FREE

It is perhaps not a surprise that ballroom movement comes from two strong individuals constantly growing and developing. One partner cannot do all the work.

While it is generally more fun to dance in partnership, it is important to realize that most of the elements that will improve your dancing are actually individual movement principals, which may and are often more effectively practiced alone. Certainly, it is your personal dedication to the improvement of your dancing as an individual that will bring your partnership forward, and any and all improvement in either partner will benefit the whole and improve your dancing together. So, the next section sets out the most important elements of individual movement in ballroom dancing. As you improve, you will spiral back on each of these elements improving each at a higher and higher level.

Partners often tend to look at improving their partner in order to improve the partnership, as any discomfort in movement is generally felt within the partnership first. However this is a distraction from where the real power to improve is - with you. It is very rare that one partner completely blocks the improvement of the other partner, and focusing on your partner's development is a waste of time, time that could be valuably spent improving you and your body, which has an immediate benefit to both you and your partnership. Finding the next way your body can improve when you cannot find any area to grow is the invaluable gift of teachers who are experienced and can see clearly the next steps forward for you when you cannot. Do not hesitate to take advantage of the resources of those who have learned what you have not, and don't get lost in trying to train someone else's horse.

That said, the following three elements will form the foundation for your personal movement. They are presented in the order that you will need to use them. Just as you get dressed before going out to meet with someone, it is best to engage all of these three elements before joining up with your partner, and, just as it works best to put on your underwear, then your pants, then your shoes, it is best to engage each of the following three elements in order. It is not possible to use element two or three without consistent use of element one and you can't fully do element three without elements one and two. So take each on one at a time. May you take them into your body and achieve everything you can imagine!

INDIVIDUAL ELEMENT 1

STAND WITH DIGNITY

OVER YOUR FEET

Beginning in Balance:

Stand with Dignity

What do we mean by dignity? Physically, it means standing taller, your spine elongated, your entire body tall from your head to your feet. It means you are at ease and confident in the world. It means you have time to do what you need to do. You have space and you take it. You have presence. You have status. You respect yourself and others respect you. You will notice that if you think of standing with dignity you will automatically stand with quite good posture.

Good Posture

Functionally, good posture is the most basic and important of all elements, which we can see by observing what happens when it is lacking or in too short supply. If one tries to dance with a posture that is compromised or understretched, one quickly finds out how difficult it is to move and how quickly we can knock ourselves off balance. It is like a waiter who has piled all his dishes on a platter in a haphazard manner. If he starts moving around the room, he will constantly have to keep trying to push the dishes back onto the platter from one direction or the next. If he had just stacked them up in an organized manner to begin with, he could have saved himself a lot of effort.

One common error is to slouch forward, your head forward and your shoulders up and over. Often, if you start this slouch, your spine will try to balance itself out by sticking out your stomach and releasing your abdominal muscles which until then had been very helpful in keeping you together as one unit. You now need to carry most of your back and body in front of you like a bag of groceries. From this position, it is so much work for your body just to stand up straight that you will be exhausted trying to move around the floor. However, if you let the top of your head rise to the ceiling as if pulled up by a puppet string, and then just engage the band of abdominal muscles between your hips slightly, like putting on a seatbelt, your spine will naturally line up the rest of your body in an efficient manner and you can move much more easily.

Another common error is for the lady to compromise her posture by reaching her body forward to try to connect to her partner. At the same time it is not uncommon for the gentleman to lean over the lady and pull her in towards his middle in an attempt to "lead", essentially pulling her off her feet, while knocking himself off his. A better option is for both gentleman and lady to stand over their own feet so they can each move themselves.

Sometimes it is not immediately visible from the outside if one has compromised ones' posture when in partnership. However, if you separate the couple and have each dance on his or her own, it will quickly become apparent if either posture is not functional. Then, each can stand up and correct his or her posture.

Vertical Spine over Foot

It is impossible to move efficiently if your weight does not travel directly over the center of each foot. Relative to the size of your foot, you are a huge mass. If a portion of this mass is to one side or the other, you will be off balance. Imagine if you wanted to move a piano on a very small rolling platform, you would not place the platform under just one corner of the piano; you would place it directly under the center. Similarly you will move best if your foot is precisely under the center of the mass that is you. Your spine runs conveniently through the center of this mass. To move efficiently, you want this spine lined up over your foot.

Sometimes dancers say "vertical" spine over foot, but what we really mean is that your spine is fully elongated and that you can feel a line through your body from the top of your head to the center of your foot. When dancing with a partner, your spine will be in actuality quite curved to make space for your partner. The spine has natural curves when it is fully elongated. As you become more advanced, you can take advantage of these natural curves to allow for more space and movement. The feeling at any level of dance, however, is always that your spine is fully stretched and your weight is over your foot.

Moving in Balance:

Clarity of Direction Through Your Feet

Of course, when you dance, you generally want to move, and if you want to move it is most helpful to decide where you are going to go before you move. Also, it is beneficial to look in the direction you are traveling. You want to choose the path which most easily enables you to accomplish everything you want to accomplish along the way. In ballroom we usually practice choreographed routines that have been rehearsed many times into habit, so that only minor effort is needed to adjust them slightly here and there if an obstacle comes in our way, and the vast majority of our attention then can be directed to the quality of each moment. It is all well and good to choose the "less traveled path", but if you change the path every few seconds, there is so much attention in path changing that it is hard to pay attention to the quality of each moment.

When moving forward your feet should always point in the direction you are moving, and you want your body to move in this direction. You want to be clear about the direction you are moving at every step. You can change direction as you are passing over a foot, but not anywhere in between; finish one step before you go to the next one. Your direction should be clear and decisive at each step. If you try going too many directions in one step or try to change directions midstep, the only thing you will achieve is to knock yourself off balance and confuse your partner. You can always make minor adjustments in distance and change directions at the next step, but the thing you cannot alter is your sense of balance, which is facilitated by moving precisely over and through your feet.

Moving from Foot to Foot

While you are traveling, it is best to travel clearly from foot to foot. What this means is that for every step you take, you would like the center of your weight to travel precisely over the center of each foot. (When standing, the center of your weight is located approximately just below your belly button, half way between the front of your stomach and your back). If we draw a line from the center of your weight to the floor, as you take a step forward, this line should travel through the center of the heel, through the middle, then through the center of the ball of each foot, approximately between your first and second toes. Similarly, if you are moving onto the ball of the foot, this line would move from the center of the back of the ball to the center of the front of the ball.

Do not try to skimp on any foot. Every step needs your full proper attention and weight. There is no need to rush. The music does not speed up or slow down. You have the time.

Head Top of Pyramid

As you take a step forward, your front ball will slide along the ground until it must flex to a heel, so both feet are constantly touching the ground. When one foot is in front of the other, there is a moment when your head is exactly half way from the back foot to the front foot, so that if you draw a line from your head straight down to the ground, it would touch the point exactly between the places where your two feet are in contact with the floor. There is a very brief moment when your weight is split exactly between both feet. Your head floats high up at the top of an evenly balanced pyramid, whose corners are your feet. The size of the base of the pyramid may vary, but your head is always centered at the very top. Remembering this feeling as you move prevents you from getting ahead of yourself and keeps you in a feeling of balance.

It should always feel like your head is either over one foot or between your two feet. Your head will never be ahead of or behind your feet, nor somewhere off to the side. It is always nicely supported over the base that is your feet.

Try:

Stand tall and elongate your spine. Feel a string pulling your head and your entire spine up to the ceiling and then placing you over the center of one of your feet. Feel your lower abdominals flatten slightly to support you.

Now try imagining that you are a tube of toothpaste and that someone squeezes you in the middle. Can you feel your spine elongating just a bit more? Feel how tall you can be. Imagine you are a king or a queen. How would you stand?

Walk a few steps forward slowly. As you walk, feel your head and spine moving over the middle of your heel, then the exact center, then the middle of the ball of each foot. Be particularly aware of the moment your head is exactly over the center of each foot. Now as you continue to walk, see if you can also notice the moment when your head and body are lined up exactly halfway between your back and front foot. Try to walk naturally. It is not the point of this exercise to try to make yourself balance, but rather to notice how balance happens naturally. Your head quite naturally balances over your elongated spine, which naturally balanced over your foot, or over the base that is formed by your two feet.

Try to remember this feeling of moving balance. Dance some familiar steps with this same awareness.

**INDIVIDUAL
ELEMENT 2**

FEEL YOUR WEIGHT AND USE IT

Feel Your Weight

To feel your weight means you have a feeling of grounding, of gravity keeping you firmly connected to the earth. You are supported by the ground beneath you, you are connected into the world. You are solid, weighted. Movement can happen on its own. You don't have to work. Gravity will do the work for you.

To feel your weight, stand tall elongating your spine. Then allow your hip and knee joints to relax slightly. If you think about relaxing into the ground, you will feel heavier and you will feel the ground holding you. Particularly if you think about the center of your weight between your hips and all the muscles around your rib cage dropping into your feet, you will get a sensation of weight.

Relaxing your muscles alone gives you a lot of weight. Have you ever tried to carry a child when he or she is asleep? It is amazing how much heavier they feel than when they are awake. You want your body to have this kind of relaxed weighted feeling into the ground around your spine which remains cleanly in line vertically over your feet. It is as if your body is a heavy fabric hanging down from a flag pole and the flag pole is secured firmly into the ground. Your head will remain high at the top of your fully elongated spine.

Another way to feel weight is to imagine you are being pulled by a giant magnet just underneath the ground, constantly pulled so that you feel almost as if you were dancing underneath the ground surface.

It is a common error for the top of our body to fall forward past our feet, gaining momentum as we move, so that eventually we are almost running. Dancing this way, if we want to suddenly reverse directions, we will have to tense our muscles to come to a rather abrupt and jarring halt. This way is rarely enjoyable or with the music. A constant poise forward becomes stressful as it is much more work to start and stop, yet, it is so habitual we often don't notice it. To break the "habitual stress position" habit requires quite a bit of deliberate attention and slowing down.

Those of us who tend to be in a rush in general often forget to take a moment to flex our hips, relax, and feel our weight into the ground before we start to move and, as a result, start running even before we have moved anywhere across the floor. If you find that you tend to rush, it helps to slow yourself down very consciously at the beginning of each dance and to bring an almost exaggerated amount of awareness as you set yourself in position and take hold with your partner to begin the dance. Listen to the music. There is plenty of time in each moment to move from foot to foot.

If we start to tense up or lock out our hip joints, we will also tend to fall forward as we begin to be pulled out of our feet, and the momentum of our top will take us away. The solution to this is to relax, allow your hip joints to bend and imagine allowing the center of your gravity to drop in your spine and into your foot. This will bring you back to a comfortably vertical moving position. It will give your flexed hips, knees and ankles the opportunity to act like shock absorbers for your movement.

The more weighted you are into the ground, the easier it is to not be knocked off your feet by random occurrences and the easier it is to recover from the rare occasions you are knocked off balance. You become like those little punching bag toys with the sand in the bottom that always come back up.

Now Use It (the Swing)

Once you can feel your weight, you now have something to swing across the floor.

A little like a golfer who swings a club, you are going to swing your entire body weight across the floor. To swing, as you take a step, allow your weight to drop into one of your legs diagonally forward into the floor. Your ankle and knee will flex, allowing the largest muscles in your leg to take your weight and assist in your momentum forward, giving you the maximum and fullest   movement,   while   your   spine   remains comfortably vertical. As your weight passes from the center of your foot to the ball, all of the muscles from your leg through your foot will be gradually activated to fully assist in your swing forward to your next foot. Concurrently, your second leg will swing forward to catch and gradually receive your weight, through the heel and then over the center of that foot.

To move backwards, you will allow gravity to compress into your standing leg and ankle, so that its knee flexes as the other leg swings back at the hip joint, toe skimming the floor behind you. The compressed leg muscles of your supporting leg can continue to facilitate the swinging motion of your body and spine backwards across the floor.

It is quite possible to dance without using the maximum benefit of gravity. You can just walk, without allowing gravity to compress your legs. This which can be done easily in harmony with your partner, but is not particularly exciting. Or, alternatively, you can muscle your way by pushing to take big steps, but this is not particularly pleasant for your partner, since it is difficult to dance in harmony and tends to create harsh, jerky movements which are not particularly suited for waltz or foxtrot. If you allow your weight to do your work for you, dancing is a much more pleasant experience. Instead of working quite so hard, you can move your attention instead to playing with the music and enjoying the dance.

My coach had been talking about weighted movement for quite a few years when one day suddenly my muscles relaxed enough to feel my weight into the ground. It was a strange phenomenon. I did feel very stable and solid into the ground, but at the same time, I suddenly felt my upper body could go any direction at all and that there was no way possible I could be knocked off balance. Further, the relaxation and freedom of my joints suddenly allowed me a heightened sensation of my partner and of the floor. It was much easier to accommodate all my partner's movement, and it was quite easy to flow around into whatever space he was not.

Weight generated movement is much more powerful than any other methods of movement. Gravity is quite a strong force and your physical weight is significant.

Breathe out, relax and allow your weight to go towards the ground at every swing. You will effortlessly travel twice the distance of those who are walking or trying to force their way through their movement.

Gravity is literally a "higher power"; it is always there to bring you back to where you want to be, on the ground. If you feel lost in your dancing and everything seems out of control, relax and bring your awareness back to your weight. The ground is something you can always depend on and come back to moment after moment after moment.

Sway and Curved Movement

As we begin to allow our weight to power our movement, we have considerably more energy moving across the floor. If we allow our bodies to sway slightly into turns (like a bike or motorcycle does as it goes around a corner) we can accommodate centripetal force in an efficient manner and use the momentum of our turn to its best advantage.

Sway is also helpful to gracefully redirect our energy to change directions or to stop our progression across the floor somewhat like skaters braking into a turn. The degree of sway that is necessary to redirect your movement to keep yourself in balance while moving will depend on the amount and speed with which you are traveling around the floor.

There is a point approximately two inches below your belly button, between the back and front of your body which we can call your lower center. When you are moving with little to no curve or sway, your lower center will move vertically in line over your foot. During a sway, your lower center will naturally swing slightly past your foot either to the side, front, or back as you curve or redirect your movement. In either case, however, the feeling will always be that your weight is moving very strongly and precisely through your feet and into the ground.

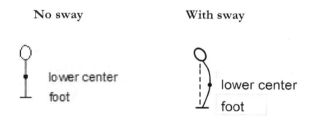

Try:

Feel your weight

Stand on your left foot and elongate your spine. Feel
your head rise to the ceiling, and engage your lower
abdominals slightly to put on your abdominal seat belt.
Relax your hip joints. Relax the muscles around your
hips and see if you can feel an increase of weight into
your left foot. Relax the muscles around your rib cage.
Pour out any tension from your back, neck, and arms
into a funnel down your spine and into your foot.

Swing forward and back exercise

Preparation back:

Elongate your spine and partially step back rising up
onto the ball of your right foot, knee slightly flexed,
leaving the left leg in front of you so that the toes of
your left foot touch the floor about two feet ahead of
you. Your head should be approximately halfway
between front and back feet.

Swing forward:

Now let your weight swing diagonally forward into
your left foot, your left ball and heel lowering to collect
your weight. Breathe out as you swing down. As your
weight continues to swing into your left hip joint, allow
your free right leg to swing forward and the ball of right
foot to slide forward until your right leg and foot

extend, your right heel touching the floor. As your spine and weight continue to swing forward over your right foot, allow your weight to continue to move forward through your right hip and foot. As your weight passes over your right foot, swing your hips and left leg forward and up so that you move onto the left ball (your left heel will not touch the ground). Your right leg remains extended behind, toe touching the floor approximately two feet behind you. As you swing up, breathe in.

Swing back:

Now, allow your weight to swing diagonally back and down compressing into the right toes, ankle, foot, knee and hip, as you let your left leg swing fully back behind you, the tip of your left big toe skimming the floor. Continue to move your body back with the underside of your right hip and thigh and compressed right leg until your body is collected over your left ankle, compressed knee and hip. Swing your right leg back and continue to move back up onto the ball of the right foot, your left leg remaining forward, left toes touching the ground approximately two feet ahead of you.

Swing forward again, your ball of left foot, heel, ankle knee, then hip collecting your weight into your next forward swing. Continue to swing forward and back.

After approximately twenty swings, repeat the same exercise on the other side, starting on your right foot. As you do these exercises, see how much you can allow your body to relax around your spine and how much you can feel the center of your weight swinging freely without muscular effort. See how much you can smooth out your movement forward and back.

BE FLEXIBLE AROUND YOUR SPINE

Free Rotation

We have already begun to discuss the importance of releasing tension in order to feel and use your weight. It is also important to note the importance and advantage of flexibility around your spine to accommodate the infinite moment to moment changes of the dance - of your body's movement, your partner's movement, and the changing situations and challenges of navigating around other couples in the room. By flexibility, I mean not out-of-the-ordinary flexibility like putting your foot behind your head, but rather just free and effortless movement around the spine. For instance, if someone poked the front of your shoulder, if your muscles are free, your side would easily swing back rotating around your spine. If the muscles and joints in your back are fixed or held, your entire back becomes one fixed block, and if someone pokes your shoulder, instead of freely rotating, the entire block tips back, and you fall over backwards.

Counterbalancing your own Movement

Your shoulders and sides quite naturally move forward and back around your spine in opposition to your legs and feet when you walk. You will find that the more places you can allow your sides, shoulders and arms to move naturally in opposition to your legs and feet while you dance, the easier it is to balance. If you dance basic figures by yourself, you can experiment with this. Allow your sides to move where ever they want to go in various movements and you will find that in places where it was previously difficult to balance, you can now balance out your own movement within your body. If you extend this feeling of flexibility and freedom into all your joints, you will find you can actually move in many ways you had not anticipated.

Now, if you allow yourself to use this flexibility particularly from the waist up) with the same sense of elongated spine we spoke about in the first chapter and at the same time feel your weight solidly into the ground through your feet as you drop your weight clearly through each foot, you will move powerfully, fluidly and in balance.

If, on the contrary, you are rigid or you fix the muscles around your spine, you will find that you will lose both fluidity and power, as even the smallest unexpected events can knock you off balance. Once you get off balance, you will tend to contract your muscles to pull yourself back on your feet to control the situation. This of course will be at the expense of both your individual movement and the movement of the couple.

Living Arms and Hold

It is common for dancers to tense up the moment they take hold with their partner. They often stiffen their entire upper body, chest, arms and neck with the mistaken idea that this will help keep the connection with their partner safe and secure. At first, from the outside of the partnership, it does appear that the connection or hold between couples is a fixed, constant, unchanging and definable thing, so it is perhaps not surprising that when we get into partnership we immediately try to set the connection. In reality, however, the hold between partners is always changing and moving, every moment, adjusting to the ever changing movement of the individuals. So, our arms need to be flexible and in tune with both our movement that of our partners.

To achieve this, your arms will feel like extensions of the flexible muscles around your spine and back. When your arms rise to take hold with your partner, they will extend first down and then easily outward and up from your center and back, like a bird lifting its wings. There is no need to alter your own dignified posture by tensing your neck or lifting your upper shoulders in order to raise your arms to connect with your partner. Your arms can easily float out from your center and back. Your arms, hands, and fingers should feel alive. You will feel energy in your arms that will extend from your body through your arms and hands, and when you take hold, to your partner.

Redirecting Energy

Besides making your balance more resilient, allowing your muscles to be flexible around your spine has the advantage that it is much easier for you to redirect your movement if you suddenly would like to change directions. If unanticipated obstacles suddenly block your way, you can fluidly redirect your movement in other directions. Also, within the partnership , the more fluid and flexible each partner, the more any unintended actions can be dissolved and redirected. Like in Aikido, you can easily redirect energies around you.

"Get Loose"

It was an interesting breakthrough in my dancing when my coaches instructed me to forget everything I had learned about look and shape and to just allow my entire top (around my spine) to be as loose as possible, to be "loosey goosy". If I felt my partner "break our line" i.e. drop my arms down, etc, or do anything odd, I was to go with it completely. Relative to my previous dancing, I felt somewhat like a ragdoll and like I was moving all over the place, but my coach was quite excited about my development. From the outside, our appearance looked cleaner, bigger and our connection appeared more still and peaceful. Two days later at a competition, we won in our division for the first time, placing over three competitors who had always placed higher than us.

I should note that my coaches gave me this more extreme instruction only after eight years of dancing with my partner, after years of instructing me not to "glue myself " to him, of telling me to dance over my own feet regardless, even if we had a gap between our bodies, to dance over my own feet so that at this point, no matter hsow loose and flexible various parts of me moved, I was habitually weighted and over my own feet.

Fluidity

With flexibility and freedom of movement naturally comes fluidity. We can say that from the time we start dancing, we never stop moving - movement is just constantly redirected throughout the body to varying degrees so that dancing feels like a continuous flow. This kind of dancing is always easier to follow for the lady as she can feel direction constantly communicated through various parts of the gentleman. When there are many starts and stops, at each stopping point she may have to guess where he is going next. With fluid motion, she gets a continuous flow of information, rather that a morse code style of blurts and blips of movement to decode, which is rather difficult to do at high speeds.

Flexibility also goes hand in hand with weightedness. Namely, the more you can allow your muscles and joints to move freely, the more your weight can drop into the ground. Also the more you drop your weight into the ground, the more you free your upper body to move around wherever it likes. And just as weightedness cannot be achieved without releasing unnecessary tension, maximum flexibility and fluidity cannot be achieved without your weight.

Try:

Stand with both knees and hips flexed. Look at one point across the room. Elongate your spine. Fix your head and hips in one place. Now swing your rib cage and arms freely around your spine. If you keep your head and hips still, how freely can you rotate around your spine?

Now relax your shoulders and slowly raise your arms so that can you feel them extending out from your back and bring them into an imaginary hold with a partner. Again swing your rib cage and arms freely around your spine. Is your neck relaxed and free?

Ask yourself when practicing on your own:
How fluidly can I move? How much can I move around my own spine while staying over my own feet? How far can I go in any random direction by balancing things out within my own body?

PUTTING TOGETHER THE ELEMENTS
OF INDIVIDUAL MOVEMENT

If you put together the elements we have discussed so far - a dignified posture moving with a clear direction through your feet, a feeling of swinging your weight, and flexibility and easy rotation around your spine, you now have a very balanced, powerful and free individual.

PART THREE

HARMONIOUS MOVEMENT WITH A
PARTNER: AWAKEN AWARENESSES

Partnership awareness is how we get harmony in movement with our partner.

We spoke in the Preparation section about the two parts of your mind - the part of your mind that is actively telling something or someone to do something and the part that is listening and picking up information. When you enter into partnership, it is the development of this second listening part that is most important. You really have very little control over your partner's movement, but you do have a choice about the degree to which you are aware of his or her movement, as well as the degree to which are aware of and clearly communicate your own movement.

In the next section we explore the three areas of awareness that help us notice our partner and thus to find ways to move in harmony with him or her.

**PARTNER
AWARENESS 1**

A LISTENING TOUCH

Connecting Nervous Systems

In ballroom dancing, sight is used only peripherally to be aware of your partner as each dancer faces away from the other. Partner awareness comes through touch, primarily from hands (the gentleman's left hand to lady's right hand, man's right hand to lady's scapula, lady's left hand to gentleman's right bicep). Full body connection will occur if both partners are dancing fully their own parts and timing their movements with each other. It should not be sought out artificially as this will disrupt posture. (Even world champions do not have full body connection when they start their practice.) It should be clear that though the point of contact and information transfer is through the hands, it is not that the gentleman intentionally communicates or moves the lady with his arms or hands. On the contrary, it is the solid movement of his entire being (body, arms, legs, weight) through his feet which is felt by the lady. He is completely connected as one unit: his hands are connected to his arms, which are extensions of his back which is connected to his strong center (or abs) which moves solidly through his feet. So, really it is just that the lady is plugging into an entire nervous system when she touches the gentleman's left hand, and because of the many nerves in our hands, she can now feel everywhere he moves.

It is an interesting paradox that if the gentleman thinks of leading with his hands he will tend to disconnect his arms from his own body and muscularly tend to start pushing and pulling the lady, at which point she automatically tenses up and struggles to regain her balance, shutting down receptive lines of communication in her body. Whereas, if on the contrary, he thinks of listening with his hands to hear where the lady is, what she feels like, where her weight is, suddenly his nervous system connects and she can feel everywhere he is going and intends to go. It is by listening that he is best and most clearly heard - and without physical effort.

Try:

Face your partner. Raise your hand. Feel your arm as an extension of your back. Feel the relationship between your hand and the center of your weight just below your belly button. Feel your weight into the ground. Now take your partner's hand. Feel its texture, amount of tension, temperature. See if you can awaken all of the senses in your hand, and see what else you can feel.

Hold your partner's hand. Ask your partner to move slowly from foot to foot. Close your eyes, and see if you can match his or her movement exactly side to side. Can you feel what part of the foot your partner is on? Switch roles and do the same with your partner closing his or her eyes.

If you take ballroom hold, can your other hand have the same level of awareness on your partner's back or arm? Do the exercise again in dance hold, with heightened awareness of your hands' contact with your partner.

A SEEING CENTER

Upper Center Oriented Towards Partner

When you enter into partnership, a portion of your attention and body orientation connects to and stays with your partner. If you had a giant eye 2-3" just below your sternum in front of your heart, it would be looking towards your partner at all times. We will call this your upper center to distinguish it from your lower center which is usually quite a bit lower, below your belly button. Even if in certain positions you are both moving to the side, as in promenade position, you always have your partner in at least peripheral awareness. Where ever you move, in whatever direction you go, your upper center will always "see" your partner.

One way to envision how moving partnerships work is to take two tennis balls. Break a pencil, so that you have a 1" section of pencil. Now glue or tape each end surface of the pencil to a tennis ball. (It will look like an old fashioned barbell.) We will call the glued point of the tennis ball, its upper center. Now you have two bodies with their centers permanently pointing towards each other.

These tennis balls can be pushed in a line, one in front of the other (linear movement)

or rolled along the floor side by side (movement in promenade position).

You can put your finger on one ball, and push the other in a circle around it (rotary figures),

or you can push both balls, pushing one more than the other (curved figures)

These objects are able to move in many ways without ever losing their center to center orientation. Like a periscope, your upper center will always be pointed towards your partner.

Inside and Outside of a Turn

When we curve or rotate in partnership, it is natural that one partner is moving more than the other. In some figures, one partner may be almost a fixed point while the other is tracing quite a large curve around him or her. It is important in these figures for the person who is on the inside of the turn, i.e., moving less, to monitor the pace and turn of the partner on the outside of the turn, who is moving more. This inside person will be providing most of the power for the partnership at this point and acting like an anchor for the other's movement.

Purely rotary figures are like someone throwing a discus. The partner who is the thrower needs to stay partially pointed towards his own hand and discus (his partner). If his body rotates faster than the hand with the discus moves around his body, he will leave the discus behind and lose power. On the contrary, if he uses his body like an anchor and rotates his body so that it is always partially pointed towards his discus, he will throw with quite a bit of power. This is not to say that the partner on the inside of the turn will be throwing his partner around him, but it is to say that if the inside person provides a stable anchor and orientation towards the partner on the outside of the turn, the person on the outside can practically fly around the turn with very little effort. As we take turns anchoring each other's movement, we can produce much more power as a couple than either of us could produce as individuals.

Try:

Stand facing your partner slightly offset to the left with knees and hips slightly flexed, weight on both feet. Your partner will do the same. Place your hands on the back of your partner's shoulder blades from either underneath or above his or her arms, so that your upper centers are facing each other. Rotate around your spines and experiment how much you can turn with your upper centers still pointing towards each other. Try moving in and out of promenade position with this hold and feel how much rotation you will need to maintain your upper center to upper center orientation.

Now dance through your normal routines. This exercise will tend to restrict your movement somewhat, but will give you clear physical feedback of at which points in the dance your upper center tends to rotate away from your partner. These are the moments in your choreography that will need the greatest attention to enable you to continue to "see" your partner.

Make sure all of your joints are as free and flexible as possible around your spine and try it again.

Now try dancing in regular hold with this new awareness.

**PARTNER
AWARENESS 3**

MY SPACE/YOUR SPACE

Invite your Partner by Giving Space

It is natural that we would not run headlong into a wall. This is because we acknowledge that the wall has integrity and it would not be helpful either to the wall or to us to run into it. Instead, it would be more prudent to just walk around or beside it. Awareness of your partner's space and movement trajectory has the same result. If you are truly aware of your partner's physical being, the space she takes up, and her movement, you will not run into or block her, but will instead move around her as she will around you, and you will each facilitate greater movement for the other.

As you move closer together to set up to dance, it is important that each person takes the personal space he or she needs to move comfortably and at the same time invites their partner by giving them the space he or she needs. Specifically in ballroom this means the amount of leftward poise, or tilt, and rotation in the upper body that feels most functional in movement. From the outside observer, this looks like the amount of space between the heads of the two partners, but, in actuality, this is an entire blob of space in which each person is free to move in counterpoint to his or her partner. Developing a sense of what this is and what is needed requires some trial and error.

A shorthand version of how to take your space in partnership is the following: stand facing your partner with your hips and shoulders parallel to your partner's hips and shoulders. Now each move slightly to you left so that your right foot points between your partner's feet. Flex your hips and transfer your weight completely to one foot (woman's left, man's left leg). Lower your left hip very slightly more than your right, your weight still over the center of your supporting leg. Rotate your head so that you face slightly to your left. Point your upper center (just underneath your sternum) towards your partner's upper center. Now you are slightly offset from each other and each should have room to move. Once you begin to move across the floor, you can take more space as you find ways to stretch diagonally.

Poising your upper body and rotating your shoulders slightly left away from your partner has the added benefit of actually physically bringing your center closer to your partner, as your body counter balances itself to be balanced over its foot. If, instead, for example, the gentleman leans over to his right or rotates his shoulders rightward, his right side will automatically be pulled away from her and give no surface for her body to connect to.

If you were to put two soap bubbles together, there is a moment when they link, before they merge when they are both flexible, and along one surface they are touching. It is as if each person is in one of these touching soap bubbles. It is best to avoid leaning over or onto your partner's bubble or pushing into it. As you move across the floor, you can feel how your bubble moves in space and changes shape in relation to your partner. You can play with how much you can stretch your own space in relation to your partner.

To develop this spacial awareness, it is helpful to first imagine the physical forms your two bodies take as you first take hold and to imagine where and how you want to move next in space. Give yourself and your partner the space needed and you will both be more comfortable.

Move Actively into your own Space

Movement in ballroom is never completely linear, which is a good thing, since if the larger partner directs his weight with a fair amount of force directly at his partner's center, she is likely to bounce off of him much as a billiard ball will bounce off the white cue ball if hit directly on center. However, if he directs his energy to the side of her and they both rotate slightly, they accommodate each other quite well.

A natural corollary of this is that each dancer's sides must move freely around his or her spine as we discussed in the chapter on flexibility. If, for example, the man moves forward with his left side slightly forward of his right and the lady freely rotates her right side slightly back as she moves back, the tops of the two dancers will remain parallel to each other.

As you become aware of and truly take and move into your space, you may start to notice two things:

1. It is difficult to be bothered by your partner's errors and you may become even less aware of them, as your space bubble easily moves to accommodate his or her movement.

2. You are less likely to be bothered by your own errors, as there is plenty of space and time to correct them. If you are off balance one moment, you easily have the next moment to move into balance again.

Try:

While dancing in hold with your partner, one trick is this: think of yourself as a giant moveable "X" where your hands and feet are each end of the X. Since you are always maximizing this X shape, you are always individually balanced. As you dance, find where you can make these X shapes around your partner.

If you are in hold with your partner and he or she moves into one space and you are freely flexible and balanced, where is your space? Where can you move in a way that is flexible, balanced, and over your own feet?

Envision the shape of the space between you and your partner. Envision the space between your head and her head, your arm and her arm, your chest and her chest, your hips and her hips, and so forth. How does this shape change as you dance? Can you make this space feel alive?

CLARITY OF INTENTION

The Power of Intention

You can now move the way you want on your own. You are fully aware of your partner's movement. Now there is only one more element you need to achieve everything you want in partnership and that is to answer this question: "What do you want to do with the skills you have today?" This is an important question and one we often forget to ask ourselves. However, it is the very asking of this question and the answering of it that is the final ingredient that magically seals the rough edges of our partnership and that brings it to life. We can call the answer to this question clarity of intention.

By clarity of intention, we mean, big picture, what do you what to achieve? Do you want to embody the music? Do you want to make beautiful shapes? Do you want to show or give a certain emotion? Is there a certain element you want to focus on or improve? What is your intention at this moment?

Sometimes it is helpful to think of a keyword to give yourself for the day that you think would be most helpful for that day's practice. If you are feeling shaky or off balance, perhaps it would be "weight." If you are feeling a lack of confidence, perhaps you would choose "dignity." You might choose a feeling word like "joy," if you want to evoke that feeling or generate that feeling in your performance. Or, perhaps you have an image in your head of an inspiring dancer 's performance, or some other image that is meaningful to you. The point is if that if you clarify a purpose for each practice, for each dance, you are much more likely to achieve this intention and you are much more likely to achieve harmony in your partnership. This is because establishing an intention, regardless of what it is, more strongly engages your mind and body with the process, and your movement becomes more conscious and alive. It reenergizes you at each moment and can counteract the tendency we all have to slip into unconscious, unwanted habitual patterns of movement.

One power of intention is that it moves you through difficulties, doubts and insecurities that may come up and may otherwise get in your way. If you have a clear intention for the day and bring your mind back to this intention if it wanders, it will act like a beacon in your dance development and bring you through places that feel uncomfortable, awkward, or forced. If you continue to bring your mind back to your intention throughout the dance, you can always succeed as you can always "intend" to do something.

Goal versus Intention

This is the difference between a goal and an intention. We do not always have absolute control over the results of our efforts with our bodies, our awareness, and our partnerships, and cannot guarantee a goal is achieved on any specific competition or even on any specific day. But, definitely if our intention is clear and our effort is consistent, over time we move farther with our intentions than we would have ever imagined with our goals. We need to keep watering the soils of our practice with our intention, practicing regularly whether it feels good or not, giving our bodies the direction they need to do what they will eventually want to do.

Performance Intention

One day I felt I was not able to dance anywhere near my normal level. I was trying to be aware in all areas, but nothing seemed to be working right. I didn't feel as an individual I could get my body to do what I wanted it to do, nor did I feel sufficiently aware of my partner. I couldn't feel my weight into the floor, my body felt tight and awkward, and I was generally frustrated. My coach, who typically gave me very specific technical feedback and thorough explanations and analogies, instructed me to " just fake it." I was surprised, but tried imagining myself performing in competition. Suddenly everything improved - my posture, my weight, my movement. Inside, I still thought I wasn't dancing the way or at the level I wanted, but my coach said that I was instantly a different dancer, and that I should dance like this all the time.

I think what happened that day when I "faked it" was not that I did something artificial, but, on the contrary, that I got out of my own way for a moment and let go of the self judgements and analysis that had been in and of themselves a distraction from my movement. At a competition or performance there is no time to analyze whether or not you or your partner is doing something right - you need to communicate something at that moment to your partner, to the judges, to your audience, regardless of the state of your mind and body that day. On that day, my intention to perform suddenly brought together the pieces I could not bring together consciously, and I much more easily embodied the shapes, images, movement and feeling I wanted to give to my audience. My body returned to a more natural way of moving and everything worked better. In this case, it was a very clear intention to perform that I needed that day.

In dance we are working to experience a feeling with our partner - harmony, connection, but, also in this competitive performance sport/art, we are trying to touch our audience and make them feel something special. Remembering this helps, especially when on occasion we get lost in the minutia of technical development, and our feeling and sensations are not what we expect, and things just don't seem to work. On these days it is helpful to take a moment to ask ourselves what we would like our audience to experience when we dance, to visualize ourselves dancing this, and then to imagine ourselves becoming our visualization. We certainly want to do this at performances and competitions. It is very common for Olympic athletes to visualize the successful achievement of their event just before they go on the field. There is no reason we should not use what has been known by high level athletes for years and to use it to our benefit every day in our practice.

The choice of what intention is best for you on a particular day is a personal one. Pick one that is exciting and motivating for you. That way the clarity of intention will act like a constant supply of gasoline to rev up your engine and energize your body when it is tired or unmotivated. You will always have something to do, something to bring you forward, and you will find it will bring your dancing to a new level of satisfaction. Whether it is a technical goal you may have for the day or a more unifying musical or performance goal, take a moment to think about and prioritize what it is that day.

Try:

To develop clarity of intention, ask yourself before each practice, what do you want? And, what do you want to achieve? Where do you want to go? Point yourself in that direction and go.

FEEL, EMOTION, & MUSIC

Feel the Music

Perhaps not coincidentally, the expression "to feel" means at once: to experience a physical sensation, to be aware, and to be able to experience emotion. As we dance we need to use all definitions of feel.

In terms of sensation, we need to feel our bodies in space, feel our weight over our feet, feel our partner's body, feel the speed, direction and amount we are each moving, and then ask ourselves how does this feel? We are developing a new much broader holistic physical awareness than we have ever had before, an awareness that is unusual in this culture, an awareness that is, relative to our previous state of awareness, superhuman.

The expression "to feel" also means to experience emotion. Though dancing with our partner brings up all sorts of emotions along the journey, the pertinent ones here are the emotions we can feel from the music and the extent to which we can allow our bodies to express these emotions through our movement.

It is possible to dance in harmony with your partner completely separate from the music, but it is much more difficult. Music provides support for the timing of your movement together, but more importantly, if you listen to the music, it reminds your body to do many things - to breathe, to relax through movements, to take time, to move fully and continuously, to enjoy the process. Dancing what the music tells us automatically brings us more in harmony with our partner.

When we talk about developing "feel" of the music, we are talking about letting our guard down enough to really hear what the music is saying to us. We are talking about allowing the music to touch us, to dance us, to breathe us. We are talking about allowing it to express something through us as dancers that is both intimately personal and universal. With all the demands of technique and other details, it is easy to forget that this is a dance we are doing. Let us not forget the magic and purity of what we are expressing!

PART SIX

THE THREE STAGES OF

DEVELOPMENT &

HOW TO DEFEAT THEIR DRAGONS

Now you know all the basic elements you will need to dance in harmony with your partner.

The next step is to put them into your body, and then to make them habits, and then to make them habits that work even under stress. Each of these steps has its own dragon that rises up in an attempt to block our way. Do not be deterred.

PUTTING NEW THINGS LEARNED INTO THE BODY

Dragon 1: Distraction

Our minds are easily distracted and easily stray from our bodies to elsewhere outside of the ballroom or to unhelpful or irrelevant things for our development - conditions in the ballroom: music too loud, other couples being annoying, little dog in the corner, our partner could be so much better if only ... so many possible distractions for our mind and we leave our body in this moment. The moment our minds are elsewhere, our body goes back to whatever old habitual patterns it is used to - sitting-in-front-of-computer posture, lack of awareness of our partner, etc.

Our society is a multitasking ADD culture of multi screened TVs, so that we can watch two different games on TV while cooking while listening to our kids.... we are so well trained to be everywhere but here, everywhere but in our body this moment. Dancing is a kind of concentration meditation for the mind. We must keep bringing it back to the moment at hand - over and over again to the principals that ultimately make things so much easier for us if we just follow them.

Defeating the Distraction Dragon: Rituals, Intention, and Focus

Make a daily ritual for what you do when you arrive in the ballroom and what you do to individually warmup. It takes a little while for our minds to come into the ballroom to join our bodies. Having a consistent warm-up ritual for your body will help bring your mind to be present. If you still find that your mind still tends to wander excessively, take longer, perhaps 40 minutes, with the body scan exercise in the last chapter or try another form of meditation some time during your day on a daily basis until you are satisfied with your concentration skills.

Then set a clear intention or focus for your practice that day. Continue to bring your mind back to that intention when it gets distracted.

When you feel something unexpected in your partnership, bring your mind back to your focus for the day, and try it again. If your dancing completely falls apart and is not coming back, separate temporarily. Try a portion of the dance again on your own. Go through your check list. Are you using all three of your individual elements to the fullest? Then try the figure alone imagining where your partner is in space and where he or she is moving. Dance it again with your partner. Is there one of the three partner awareness elements you could improve in this figure that would help? It should be remembered that when dancing in partnership you will need all three individual and all three partner awareness elements. You may have inadvertently dropped one or two and may need to bring them back in order before you continue to work on your intended focus for the day. If you get truly stuck, write a note to bring this to your next lesson with your teacher and return to your intention for the day. Try your hardest to use partner awareness elements to accommodate the movements of your partner and to refrain from judgements about your partner's movement. Problem-solving is rarely the most efficient use of time. There are much bigger and better things to do.

STAGE 2

DEVELOPING POSITIVE HABITS

Dragon 2: Silly Habits

Silly habits - we all have them. We know we have them. We stay up too late, we bite our nails, we fiddle if we are nervous. Our bad habits will try to unravel our practice, whether they are behavioral, habitual tardiness, criticism , procrastination, or physical, tense shoulders, a tendency to tip forward or back, to slouch. We all have our own personal ticks. Left to our own devices, our habits will have us do what we have always done, regardless of how many teachers tell us to do otherwise.

Defeating the Silly Habit Dragon: Repetition, Repetition, Repetition

There is only one way to fight the silly habit dragon and that is intentional concentrated awareness and Repetition, Repetition, Repetition. It is hard work to make things easy!

So, it is best to set up a regular sequence of events for your practice that you do every day for training the habits you want to have in order to replace the ones you keep coming back to. These would be the silly habits you have been told about or have noticed over and over again, but that you keep hoping will go away, since you do know about them. The new fun moves or techniques you are learning you can practice in a minute, but first take some time for the more meaningful, gradual shifts in habit that will eventually give your dancing a new foundation and will make your dance life much easier in the long run.

Think about where in your daily practice you could devote time to giving quality attention to retraining these habits. If it is an attitudinal habit you would like to change, you might want to include it in your preparation, just before your practice. If it is an ongoing physical habit, you may want to include it as part of your individual warm-up. Think about where it makes sense to dedicate this time and attention. Be patient as your body adjusts to its new and ultimately more comfortable way of dancing.

MAKING NEW HABITS RESILIENT TO STRESS

Dragon 3: Fight or Flight

As we mentioned in our chapter on preparation, our body is like a horse. As such, our body-horse is often easily spooked - a bit of wind through the leaves, a large shadow, something unusual, and it panics - such is our body. Especially in our rushed society, many of us go in and out of hyperactive emergency states throughout the day. Some adrenaline can be helpful, particularly in competition; However, we must train to use it to our advantage, because when the body goes into a fight or flight state, the typical physical responses are:

1. Tense shoulders and neck for battle (losing long dignified spine).

2. Picking up your weight out of the ground and pitching forward ready to run (losing weight and thus power).

3. Tense arms and upper body (losing flexibility around spine). Now, tense muscles cannot feel, so

4. You quickly lose sensory awareness of yourself and your partner. Unaware of where your partner is without your sense of touch,

5. You lose awareness of both space and

6. You lose the ability to be aware of your upper center orientation towards your partner.

This one state of mind has managed to disarm you of all the helpful principals you need to move with your partner. You will be in a good physical state to pick your partner up, throw him or her in a sack, and make a run for it to escape a tiger that is chasing you. But, if there is no tiger in the ballroom at that moment, your body is not in the best state for practicing harmonious movement with your partner.

Defeating the Fight or Flight Dragon:
Learn in Comfort, Train Past Stress

It is your task to identify what in the road spooks your horse - a squirrel? judges in the room? You must train your mind gently not to panic at these things. Just as you would not train your horse by making it walk through a minefield, it is best to start by removing all stressors when you train your body to do something new.

So, at first , figure out in what environment you feel most comfortable to practice, and practice what you have learned at your lessons. Do you feel most comfortable without feed-back from your partner? Perhaps you could ask to practice without talking. The main thing to remember is that initial learning of a concept cannot happen when your body is in a fight or flight state. You must train it to be calm.

Now, at the same time, in order to perform well under stress in the future, we will also need to train our minds and bodies to get used to operating under stress. A good way to do this is to schedule two very different kinds of practices, one kind, a lesson learning practice as we have described above, say four times a week, to work on basic elements of movement or concepts from your lessons under your ideal learning conditions, and a second kind of practice, a rounds or performance practice, perhaps twice a week, in which you replicate the stressful conditions you are likely to encounter.

In a rounds practice, you would like to set up the conditions as close as you can to the stressful situation you will likely dance in. If it is a competition, it is ideal to try to practice with other dancers in a scheduled rounds practice, where you dance all of your routines without stopping and you have people in your way. If it is not possible to practice with others, imagine others on the floor and play the music for your dances one after the other without stopping.

You should not talk to your partner during your rounds. Both you and your partner should understand that the quality and comfort of your dancing will diminish considerably at first during these practices, but this is normal. If you dance all of your dances again, even if they feel horrible, and then dance them even again, they will eventually feel better.

Once your body and mind get accustomed to these kinds of practices, there will be less of a loss of the quality you feel in your lesson practices, and you will feel much more confident when you encounter the actual competition. If you are able to accept some discomfort on occasion, you will be much happier in the long run.

PART SEVEN

A SAMPLE DAILY PRACTICE

A Practice Structure to Train Past the Dragons

The following is a sample practice structure using the principals of this book. It is the structure that my partner and I have used that has worked well for us over the last ten years. My partner and I practice six days a week (four lesson practices, and two rounds practices) in conjunction with our private lesson with our teacher once a week. We compete in Latin American dancing as well, so our structure must save time and energy for practicing Latin dancing after our ballroom practice.

If you have not already read it, an excellent book to assist in structuring your practices and clarifying and meeting your dance goals is *Dance To Your Maximum* by Maximilian Winkelhaus. This book provides information on all areas of development as a dancer, including how to prepare your mind during practice and before and during competition.

Your practice plan is personal and should fit what you would like to achieve with your dancing. Discuss your goals with your dance teacher and partner and come up with a practice plan and structure that fits you.

The amount of time, energy, and focus you chose to devote to your dancing practice will determine your rate of progress.

Sample Practice Structure

1. Preparation (10 minutes)

2. Individual swinging warm-up (10 - 20 minutes)

3. Partner awareness warm-up (10 minutes)

4. Lesson learning practice (60 - 90 minutes) and/or

5. Rounds or performance practice (30 minutes)

6. Practice log (5 minutes)

1.

PREPARATION

(10 minutes)

Body scan exercise

Sit in a quiet space where you will not be disturbed - a car works well. Set a timer for 10 minutes. Sit very tall. Close your eyes and take several deep breaths. Feel the oxygen filling your chest and body and your body relaxing with each exhale.

Bring your mind to a point at the top point of your head and scan downwards to see what you can sense. Feel your scalp, your forehead, your eyes, ears, nose, inside your mouth. See if you feel any sensations in your head, such as pressure, tingling, any pain. Allow any tension to be released as you gradually move your awareness down your body. If you find tension and it does not release, just notice it. Briefly inquire whether there are other feelings there - heat, cold, pain? Then continue to move your attention downward. Feel your neck and shoulders, upper back, and inside your chest. See if you can feel the skin on the surface of your body and feel the muscles underneath the skin. Continue moving your awareness down your body through your arms and hands, then hips, thighs, knees, calves all the way through your ankles, feet, and toes.

Once you have touched every part of your body with your mind, see if you can experience the entire inside of your body as one space. See if you can feel what shape this body is making at this moment.

Once your 10 minutes is up, open your eyes and move your body around slightly, wiggling your fingers and toes. Try to continue to feel the whole shape of your body moving.

Clarify your intention

Take a few moments to think about what your ideal practice would look like. Briefly visualize each part of the practice the way you would like it to be, how you would like to dance, what specifically you would like to achieve, how you would like to experience your practice in the ideal of all possible worlds.

Now you both have a sense of what is going on with your body today and you have a clear map of where you are going. You can enter the ballroom.

2.

INDIVIDUAL SWINGING WARM-UP

(10 - 20 minutes)

Activate the three individual elements:

Stand with dignity over your feet

Dancing on your own, swing forward and back (see the exercise at the end of Part 2.2) at first only thinking of one thing, the principal of standing with dignity, i.e. elongated vertical spine over your feet. Ask your body to do this and listen to what it feels like and is actually is doing. Is it in line? As you swing forward does a line from your head to the ground move through the center of each foot? Can you feel your head over the base that is formed by your two feet or over one foot ? As you swing and your mind goes elsewhere, bring it back. Check your spine. Check your head in relation to your feet.

Feel your weight and use it

Then as you swing forward and back, think of feeling your weight. Let your hip joints relax and swing. Does your swing get deeper and fuller as you relax? Once again, as your mind wanders, bring it gently back to feeling your weight. Listen back and forth, feel your spine over your feet, then feel the fullness of your weight moving smoothly forward and back.

Flexibility around your spine

When you feel like your spine is moving consistently and vertically over your feet and your weight is swinging smoothly from foot to foot, feel your rib cage and arms and swing them gently around your spine. Can you relax your muscles around your spine more so that you can allow more weight to swing down into your feet?

It usually takes me about 20 swings on each side for me to fully unravel the extraneous tension and body patterns of the day and to feel the simplicity of my spine swinging over my feet.

Dance some around the room on your own with your arms relaxed and free by your sides. Feel where naturally your upper body wants to rotate around your spine to counter your movement across the floor. Now, allow your arms to rise easily from your back into approximately the height they would be to be in hold with your partner. Dance through several walls of your dances with the same flexible feel in your arms and back as you had when your arms were relaxed by your sides.

When you feel all three individual elements clearly active in your body, you are fully "dressed" and ready to meet your partner. We will need to keep all of these elements active while we are in partnership.

3.

PARTNER AWARENESS WARM-UP

(10 minutes)

Individual element review and awaken three partner elements

Your partner warm-up consists of specific opportunities to remind your mind and body of both partner and individual elements.

A. Walk Towards Your Partner

Recall your individual elements - dignity, weight, flexibility

Just before and in between dances is a great opportunity to bring back your individual principals. As you are walking to meet your partner, breathe in deeply and feel the oxygen elongate your spine and enliven your upper body. Let your upper body and arm shake a little to let go of any tension from the last dance and loosen up for the next one. Then as you stand facing your partner, feel your weight settle into the ground.

B. Set Up - Taking Hold in Partnership

Awaken all individual and partner awarenesses

Traditionally, the gentleman takes his place on the floor first, the lady comes to the gentleman, and then the gentleman adjusts to the lady. Functionally, the set up would work well with either partner starting, as long as whoever starts also takes the time to readjust to his or her partner once the partner joins them in hold. It is helpful on occasion to reverse who starts the set up so that each can notice what is the most comfortable starting position for the other.

To begin your warm-up with your partner, perform three set-ups of your first dance (waltz), going through each of the focuses in the following chart:

THE SET-UP

Man	Woman
Think "Dignity, Weight, Flexibility"	**Think "Dignity, Weight, Flexibility"**
Dignity - Lengthen your spine and stand precisely over the center of your right foot.	*Dignity* - Lengthen your spine and stand precisely over the center of your left foot
Weight -Allow all tension and your weight to settle into the ground, flexing your hip joints	*Weight* -Allow all tension and your weight to settle into the ground, flexing your hip joints
Flexibility-Feel your muscles free around your spine and your arms as flexible extensions of your back.	*Flexibility*-Feel your muscles free around your spine and your arms as flexible extensions of your back.
Think "Center, Touch, Space"	**Think "Center, Touch, Space"**
Center - Point your upper center towards your partner	*Center* - Point your upper center towards your partner.
Space - Envisioning where you will be moving next in space, make space for the woman with a slight poise and rotation left. Make sure your weight is still securely into the floor.	*Space* - Envisioning where you will be moving next in space, step in parallel to the man's right side and resettle your weight through the center of your left foot, taking your comfortable space stretched left.
Touch - Reach out to invite her with your left listening hand, your arm an extension of your back.	*Touch* - Take the man's left hand with your right listening hand, your arm an extension of your back.

Man	Woman
Think " Space, Touch"	**Think "Touch"**
Space - Mold your space to the woman's space, so that both are comfortable.	
Touch - Place your right hand on the lady's back with a listening right hand.	*Touch* - Place your left hand on the inside of the man's right bicep with a listening left hand.

C. Warm Up Walls

You will now dance through all walls of your dance choreography for each dance, one wall at a time without talking. Individually, choose one specific focus for this exercise, a habit you would like to retrain or the individual or partner awareness element you feel needs the most work for you at this time. If you have don't know what to choose, ask your teacher or partner for their preference. Now, dance one wall at a time of each dance with your partner bringing your attention to this focus. At the end of each wall, stop to detach from your partner and re set-up for the next wall, bringing back to your awareness each six elements in each set up, as discussed in the previous section. Then recall your chosen focus for the day and dance your next wall. When you get to tango, perform three tango set ups before you begin this dance to remind your body of the correct tango position and how all six elements feel in this dance. Dance through all of your routines one wall at a time.

It is important not to talk during your warm-up walls. This is a time when each partner is bringing back awarenesses into his or her body; our bodies are still waking up, so they are not yet ready to discuss or to learn something new. It is tempting to try to help your partner, but as neither of you is fully yet in your body, your well-meaning attempts will be counter-productive at this time of your practice.

4.

Lesson/Learning Practice

(60-90 minutes)

Making the most of your lessons

It is helpful to have a dance lesson with your teacher at least once a week and to take notes after every lesson. Your notes will prove invaluable the next day in practice, when you are recalling and trying to reproduce all that you learned in your lesson.

As we mentioned, you should have a weekly schedule, so that you have some lesson practices and some rounds practices. In your lesson practice, take a moment to review the notes you have taken from your most recent lesson with your teacher. Take a moment to remember the feeling your body had when you were dancing in your lesson. Review any notes you have taken from last practice. Then coordinate with your partner what material you would like to practice. You can go through your lesson notes one by one if they are individual, specific corrections. Or, if your would like to improve on one of the elements of this book or another subject such as use of feet, sway, or expression, you can dance through your dances one or two walls at a time with your chosen subject. During the lesson practice, you may want to talk with your partner as you help each other recall what you learned in your lesson and which parts you want to improve.

If you practice something several times and you are not able to make the improvements you felt in the lesson, move on the next item to practice, and make a note to bring the figure back to your teacher. As we have mentioned, the most productive practices are those in which each individual continues to work on improving elements within his or her own body and on improving awareness versus focusing on problem solving between partners.

5.

Rounds Practice

(30 minutes)

Preparing for performance

If you have time you can practice rounds on the same day as your lesson practice, or you can practice your rounds on a separate day from your lesson practice. For your rounds practice, review any notes you have taken from previous rounds. In particular, review what old bad habits tend to try to reemerge for you personally under stress. Visualize yourself moving with your new chosen habits at those moments instead.

Take the floor for your performance. Pretend that you have an audience. Pay attention to how you present yourself coming on and off the floor and in between dances, and choose how you would like to be seen by your audience.

When the music starts, truly listen. Remember that you are an extension of its expression. Dance your first dance. During the ten second break between dances, breathe and refocus your mind on what you intend to do in the next dance. Dance all of the dances in your round. Bow to acknowledge your fictitious audience.

When you are done dancing five dances, each partner

can jot down notes for each dance. It is best to continue to refrain from talking for at least five minutes, after which, adrenaline has settled and each partner can share his or her notes with the other. Dance the round again and try to improve on the items you or your partner noticed. Take notes again and dance a third round.

6.

Practice Log

(5 minutes)

At the end of each practice, take a brief moment to jot down the date, amount of time you practiced, any insights and successes you have had, things to work on for your next practice and any questions you have for your teachers.

Congratulate yourself and your partner on a great practice. Dance practice is difficult, but rewarding work. Bring your improved skills and awareness with you into the rest of your life as you leave the ballroom.

CONCLUSION: DEVELOPING FEEL

You are now very familiar with the three individual movement principals and three partner awarenesses necessary to dance in harmony with your partner. You understand the importance of mindful preparation, feeling the music, and setting a clear intention for your practices. You are aware of the potential dragons to progress, and you know how to both develop and gradually strengthen your skills so that you can move in harmony under even the most stressful situations.

Integrating Sensations and Awareness

As you practice more and more, you will gradually begin to experience how the three individual movement elements and three partner awarenesses work together, and you will develop a feel of how to move more and more efficiently by yourself and with a partner. The more you can consciously experience and sense how your entire body feels when it is moving correctly (or even when it is not moving correctly), the more quickly you will learn. Of course, the more often you are able to reproduce the feeling of efficient movement, the easier it is to reproduce it in the future.

When things don't feel as ideal as you would like, you will become more skilled at going through the checklist and checking if perhaps one of the six elements has been forgotten or has fallen out of your awareness. You will know which element would be best to focus on to bring you back into your sense of balance, power, and freedom as an individual and/or back into harmony with your partner. You will increasingly feel the support and energy of the music as it becomes more and more your guide, and you will become better at intuitively knowing what is the best intention to set for that day.

Six elements may seem like many things to have in your awareness at one time, which is why we recommend that each day you bring them back into your body, layering them one by one, and that you fully have all of your individual movement elements working for you in your body before you take on the three additional awarenesses you will need to dance with a partner. Over time, you will gradually experience them as one feeling, one that feels efficient and right, and it will be harder to go back to less efficient ways of moving and less conscious levels of partner awareness.

We know that once we have begun to feel these principals working for us in our body, we need to practice them and bring our attention back to them over and over again until they become habitual and more and more clear. All six principals need daily tending and care and our intention will need to be renewed daily.

Your dance relationship is a living and thriving thing and, with deliberate attention, it will grow in all areas and become fuller and more harmonious as you as an individual become more balanced, powerful and free. The result will be a feeling of connection, not because you are holding on to each other, but by timing with each other and moving in harmony. It is an ever moving and changing connection, born out of habitual awareness of and thus respect for the others autonomous shape and movement.

Enjoy your dancing!

RECOMMENDED READING

Cameron, Julia. *The Artist's Way*. New York:, Penguin Putnam, 1992

Hearn, Geoffrey. *A Technique of Advanced Standard Ballroom Figures*. London: Geoffrey and Diana Hearn, 2007

The Imperial Society of Teachers of Dancing. *The Ballroom Technique*. London: The Imperial Society of Teachers of Dancing, 1948. Reprinted with amendments, 1994

Gawain, Shakti. *Creative Visualization*. Novato, California: Nataraj Publishing, 1978

Jarmolow, Diane with Brandee Selck. *Teach Like a Pro*. United States: Diane Jarmolow, 2011

Jarmolow, Diane and Kasia Kovak with Brandee Selck. *Move Like a Champion*. United States: Move Like a Champion, Inc., 2011

Kabat-Zinn, J.E. *Full Catastrophy Living: Using the Wisdom of Your Body and Mind to Face Stress, Pain, and Illness*. New York: Bantam Dell, 1990

Kabat-Zinn, J.E. *Whereever You Go There You Are*. New York:

Bantam Dell, 1990

Moore, Alex. *Ballroom Dancing.* London: A & C Black Limited, 1936, Ninth edition, 1986

Loehr, James E. *The New Toughness Training for Sports.* New York: Penguin Books, 1994

Orlick, Terry. *In Pursuit of Excellence,* Fourth Edition, Champaign, IL: Human Kinetics, 2008

World Dance Council educational website. Edited by Ruud Vermey. http://www.wdcdance.com

Winkelhaus, Maximilian. *Dance To Your Maximum,* First Edition www.DancePlaza.com, 2001, Second Edition DanceSport International, LTD, Croydon, United Kingdom, 2011

ABOUT THE AUTHOR

Photo by Shell Jiang

Susanna Hardt is a three time United States Senior 1 ten dance ballroom and Latin champion. She owns and operates dance and creativity studio Suzie's Studio in San Rafael, California and competes and performs regularly with her husband and dance partner Todd Marsden as A Tall Order (www.talldancers.com). She gives lectures and workshops on ballroom dance and the creative process and can be reached at:

Suzie's Studio
36 Woodland Ave. Suite D
San Rafael, CA 94901
www.suziestudio.com

Made in the USA
Lexington, KY
14 February 2015